ROB HILLS

The Mindful Leadership Blueprint

A practical guide

Contents

Dedication

To my wife Bree,
and my sons Reuben and Parker . . .
My reasons to be mindful.

* * *

Preface

In today's fast-paced and ever-changing world, the need for effective and compassionate leadership has never been greater. As we navigate through the complexities of the modern workplace, the role of a leader extends far beyond traditional management skills. To truly inspire and empower our teams, we must cultivate a mindful approach to leadership that encompasses empathy, self-awareness, and an unwavering commitment to personal growth.

The Mindful Leadership Blueprint: A Practical Guide is the result of years of collective wisdom, research, and practical experience from working with leaders across various industries. It is a comprehensive resource designed to equip both seasoned and aspiring leaders with the tools and insights needed to excel in their roles while creating a positive and transformative impact on the lives of those they lead.

In the pages that follow, we will explore the fundamental principles of mindful leadership and provide practical guidance on how to apply them in your everyday leadership journey. We will delve into the importance of self-awareness, emotional intelligence, and authentic communication as pillars of effective leadership.

Throughout this book, you will discover practical mindfulness practices and exercises that will help you deepen your self-awareness, enhance your focus, and develop your ability to lead with intention and authenticity. From reflective practice to mindful decision-making, each chapter offers valuable insights and actionable steps to cultivate a mindful leadership approach that can be integrated into the way you want to lead.

Whether you are a seasoned executive, a team manager, or an emerging leader, the Mindful Leadership Blueprint will serve as your guide on the journey towards becoming a more conscious, compassionate, and effective leader. It is our hope that the wisdom shared within these pages will inspire you to embrace mindfulness not only as a leadership strategy but as a way of life.

Mindfulness, at its core, is the art of being fully present and aware in each moment, enabling leaders to make conscious choices and respond effectively to the challenges they face. There are still misconceptions around mindfulness and what it all means. This is often the reason some people don't want to know more about mindfulness, let alone apply it to their leadership. In this book, I want to tell you about mindful leadership from a practical and pragmatic viewpoint. In a way that I have taught it to people with practical backgrounds like those in Defence, Law Enforcement, Accounting, Real Estate and many more.

In this book, you won't find any mention of chanting, saying the word 'Om', burning incense, partaking in religious practices, or anything compelling you to shave your head and join a monastery. While these are all valid practices (and by no means am I devaluing those who engage in these practices), it's just not my style of mindfulness, and it's certainly not the aim of this book.

I want to present mindfulness in an easily digestible way. I want to reach those people who would benefit most from mindfulness but are reluctant to try it because they haven't found a style that suits their needs.

This book is for leaders who want a better way of leading, a healthier approach that focuses on the mental health of their people. It's a blueprint for those who don't have a mindfulness practice but are curious about how they might be able to start one. It's for leaders who sometimes put the task before the team (or themselves) at the expense of their own mental health.

I have broken the book into four parts. In Part One, I will talk about my own journey to mindfulness and give you a brief introduction to mindful leadership. Part Two focuses on 'why' and presents the business case for mindful leadership. In this section, we look at what mindful leadership is and why we should all try and integrate mindfulness into our leadership. In Part Three of the book, you will learn some of the practical tools you can use every day to become a more mindful leader. These simple but effective tools are easy to learn, and you can start applying them straight away. The final part of the book is titled What Next? and discusses what the road ahead may look like as you become a more mindful leader.

I am just a recovering other thinker on a mission to help

others be the best leaders they can be. So, I offer this book to you, not as a medical professional or mindfulness scholar, but as someone who has benefited immensely from applying mindfulness to my own leadership practice and has helped others do the same. By integrating mindfulness into your leadership toolkit, you have the power to create a ripple effect that extends far beyond your workplace, touching the lives of individuals and communities at large.

Your leadership has the potential to shape a better world, and it all begins with the choices you make in this moment. May your journey be enlightening, empowering, and filled with mindful leadership.

I

What

An introduction to mindful leadership

1

Introduction

The reason I became interested in mindfulness wasn't because it sounded fun or even particularly interesting. It wasn't even because I was jumping on the bandwagon of the latest fad or social craze (mindfulness wasn't even really 'a thing' back when I started). I came to mindfulness out of necessity, a strong internal pull to find some sort of peace from an overactive mind.

For as long as I can remember I have been an overthinker and someone who enjoys spending a lot of time alone and in my own head. As a kid, I really enjoyed doing activities alone, preferring the peace and quiet of solitude to hanging out with friends. I viewed the world from a very narrow lens by thinking there was no problem that couldn't be solved if I just spent more time thinking about it. But unfortunately thinking often leads to overthinking, which in turn can quickly become rumination. And when you ruminate, it often leads you down some pretty dark and scary holes-I have seen the bottom of my fair share of those holes.

If I hadn't found mindfulness I really don't know what impact that would have had on my mental health and ultimately how that would have played out in my life. Luckily for me, I won't ever have to find out.

My first real exposure to self-development came in the late 1990s, when my girlfriend at the time (now my wife) bought me a book that would ultimately change the course of my life. The book was called *Don't Sweat the Small Stuff, and It's All Small Stuff* by Richard Carlson. Although that might not sound like a mindfulness book, and the author didn't mention the word mindfulness once, many chapters are based on mindfulness concepts. The book really resonated with me and it showed me there was a way out of my moods, if I could just get past my need to overanalyse everything. So began a journey of personal discovery and my initial attempts at trying to get relief from my overactive mind.

When I first tried meditation it really didn't stick; I found sitting still doing nothing for long periods of time incredibly difficult. For some reason I bought into my own ridiculous reasoning that to get any benefit from meditation you needed to sit for at least twenty minutes at a time and have no thoughts whatsoever. It's no wonder I felt like such a failure when I could barely sit for two seconds without thoughts popping into my head.

So I had a few false starts, which created this love/hate relationship with meditating-I loved the idea of meditating but hated actually doing it! Those false starts rolled on for a number of years, as I couldn't turn it into a sustainable habit.

One day I came across an article that said the point of meditation wasn't to have no thoughts, the point was to focus the mind on just one thought, like a mantra or, more commonly, by following the breath. That felt more achievable to me and intuitively made much more sense.

But the real game changer came when I started to break my meditation down into smaller chunks. I threw out the old model of twenty-minute sessions and started with just one minute. I practiced over a period of weeks before slowly increasing the time as I became more comfortable with the process. That made a huge difference for me and allowed me to consistently sustain what would become a lifelong practice. I was finally able to experience the calming nature of meditation, without the frustration and self-reprimands.

My introduction to meditation and mindfulness occurred while I was serving in the Royal Australian Air Force (RAAF). In that culture, and at that time, it wasn't something I really felt comfortable talking about with my friends and colleagues. I thought if I let people know what I was doing it would draw attention to myself, and perhaps on some level, even ridicule. So I practiced in isolation and never really talked about it with anyone. That was more of an indictment of my own ego (and fear) rather than of the prevailing culture of the armed forces.

I loved my time in the Air Force, and it was a great apprenticeship for shaping my views on leadership and management. I used this time to shape my own leadership style, which was also impacted on my secret mindfulness practices.

I learnt so much-not only through the practical application of leadership but also by seeing how others in those environments chose to lead. From the stereotypical recruit instructor yelling in my face because I missed a button on my shirt at five in the morning as we stood in the freezing rain, to the wise and respected senior non-commissioned officer who led with wisdom and a more reserved demeanour.

By applying the principles of mindful leadership, I chose a less traditional style of leadership than the prevailing norm at the time. I believe this style of leadership served me well throughout my career with the Air Force, and in all of my subsequent roles. It certainly ignited a passion within me to show others that perhaps there was a better way to lead.

It wasn't until I left the Air Force and joined the Australian Federal Police (AFP) that I finally felt comfortable enough to talk about my own experiences with mindfulness and mediation. At the time I was a leadership trainer in the Leadership and Command Training Team, tasked with running leadership programs in our major offices across the country for our members. These programs included both sworn officers (uniformed, badge, gun) and professional staff (no badge, no gun, often more administrative roles), who would share their own leadership struggles in managing teams and themselves.

We of course talked a lot about different leadership principles and strategies on these programs, however the conversations that affected me the most were those regarding how these incredibly hard-working leaders often struggled to find balance or cope in high-pressure situations. As serving members of the

AFP, these men and women were often seeing the very worst of human kind, and often in very trying conditions. If anyone deserved better coping mechanisms and ways of dealing with stress in their lives, it was these dedicated people.

When I first started applying mindfulness in the workplace and then to my leadership practice, it was like turning on a switch. It quickly became clear to me that there was a better way of leading, one that felt more in alignment with my values and who I was as a person. It struck me that there was a real need for this style of leadership-not only in my workplace, but also in the culture of most workplaces.

So that led me to finally opening up more about my own experience with mindfulness and meditation. I thought that if I could share some of the strategies and techniques to help others be more mindful in intense situations, it might help in some small way to alleviate some of the suffering.

Now, if there was ever an audience who might be dubious about mindfulness it was these guys. I really had to choose my words carefully and talk about mindfulness in a practical and non-threatening way if I wanted to maintain any credibility. Despite my fear of being judged by my colleagues, I decided to speak up and share some of those experiences.

To my surprise, my fears about other people's judgments were completely unfounded. In fact, it was pretty much the opposite. People became curious about my mindfulness practice and often wanted to know what I was doing and how I was doing it.

So I started incorporating mindfulness into coaching sessions, team meetings and small group sessions, as well as the in-class discussions. I found that once we cut through the myths people thought about mindfulness, there was a real appetite for it, particularly from people in leadership roles to help relieve some of the workplace stress these people were experiencing.

I don't see mindful leadership as the panacea that will fix all leaders and any workplace issues, but it is the foundation for becoming more self-aware and deliberate in how we lead others and ourselves. In a world that is becoming more complex and changing so rapidly, it's time to revaluate leadership and what that looks like in the twenty-first century.

Trying to be more present in everything I do has made a huge impact on my life and my leadership. Being more in touch with my thoughts, my body, and my surroundings has bought a feeling of resilience and peace that no self-help book has ever managed to do. With that clarity I am able to make better decisions for those I lead, and I am better able to manage my emotions and how I interact with others.

Has mindfulness turned me into a monk who is at total peace with the world and remains serene in the face of adversity? No, but it has given me a set of tools and techniques I use on a daily basis to be more present with what I'm doing, and this has had an enormous impact on my leadership.

I still stumble from time to time-more regularly than I like to admit-however, my ability to stay focused, remain calm in stressful situations, and to be more present has made me a better leader.

Over the years I have designed ways I could use mindfulness in the workplace that retained all the benefits of the practice but didn't draw attention to myself. I wrote this book for leaders who want a practical guide to becoming a more mindful leader without jumping up on the desk in full lotus position to meditate.

This book is designed as a practical blueprint, a how to guide that will give you the strategies, tools, and techniques to apply mindfulness to your leadership today.

This book is for people who want a better workplace, not just for themselves, but also for those around them. To be a leader who places a higher importance on people rather than the bottom line (and, funnily enough, by focusing on the people in most cases we actually improve the bottom line).

My hope is that maybe together we can create a real movement of mindful leadership in the workplace.

2

What Is Mindful Leadership?

Mindfulness has arguably been around for tens of thousands of years, but it has only been in the last ten years that we have seen mindfulness gain popularity and acceptance in the modern workplace. Organisations around the world are slowly uncovering the benefits of having a more focused, engaged and resilient workforce. The research into mindful leadership alone has seen a dramatic increase over the last five years.

Mindfulness by itself is just bringing more moment-to-moment awareness into your day. It's focusing on the present moment rather than worrying about things that have happened in the past or being anxious about what may happen in the future. It's also being fully immersed in one activity rather than trying to juggle multiple things at once (and usually not doing any of them particularly well!).

The simplest definition of mindful leadership is the application of mindfulness principles to the practice of leadership. It's self-awareness and the ability to self-regulate in difficult situations. It's a presence in how you interact with others and how you give them your attention. Being a mindful leader is more than just showing up, it's about being truly present in all situations.

But it's so much more than that, and I will show you that throughout this book.

Now, no mindfulness book would be complete without referencing the modern-day father of mindfulness, Jon Kabat Zinn. He says, 'Mindfulness is paying attention in a particular way; on purpose, in the present moment, non-judgmentally'[1].

What really stands out for me about this quote are the three characteristics of mindfulness and how we can apply them to leadership:

1. **On purpose:** Who are we leading, and what is our leadership for? What do we want our leadership legacy to be? Are we proactive in the way we approach leading our teams?

2. **In the present moment:** Too much of our lives is spent worrying about things that have happened in the past which we can no longer do anything about or fretting over something that may never even come to fruition-a meeting that went wrong, or a project that missed the mark, a big presentation we are dreading, or a difficult conversation we keep putting off.

3. **Non-judgmentally:** We are constantly judging, whether it is ourselves, other people, or the situation. We add layers that don't need to be there. Mindfulness is about suspending

judgment and trying to accept things as they are, without the internal commentary.

The sign of a mindful leader is someone who is willing to stop whatever they are doing, no matter how busy they are, and give you their full attention. I remember the first time I noticed this many years ago with one of the senior leaders I worked for. Despite the fact I knew she was extremely busy juggling many urgent tasks, she always stopped typing on her keyboard and physically turned towards me when I entered the room to ask my questions.

I remember to this day how valued that made me feel. I felt like I was truly being listened to and that I was just as important as any of the other urgent tasks she was trying to complete.

This is something I work on whenever someone interrupts my day to ask a question or provide me with information. Sometimes I can feel the desire to keep on going, to just type a few more words, but I know the person talking to me deserves my full attention. I know the feeling they are going to get if I stop whatever it is I'm doing and just listen-they are going to feel valued too! As Susan Scott said in her bestselling book, *Fierce Conversations*, 'While no single conversation is guaranteed to change the trajectory of a business, a career, a marriage, or a life, any single conversation can[2]'. We have to be willing to be there for every conversation because we never know when that life-changing conversation may happen.

Although the focus of this book is on becoming a more mindful leader, a lot of what I write about can easily be applied to your everyday life. You shouldn't just aim to be mindful for eight hours a day at work and then come home and switch to autopilot. Mindfulness needs to be woven into the entire tapestry that makes up your life.

With that in mind I will also be writing about things that don't just happen during the nine-to-five workday. These topics-like waking up, setting a daily intention, and managing the transition between work and home-are just as important as the things that happen during working hours to becoming a mindful leader.

3

Why Mindful Leadership?

Not only does there seem to be more scientific research available daily about the benefits of mindfulness, I also seem to be hearing a lot more anecdotal evidence as well. People send me emails or stop me in the hallways to tell me how these practices are making them better leaders in the office and at home.

One of the main reasons I started applying mindfulness to my leadership was the way it always seemed to help me feel more centred, even in the midst of whatever crazy situation the day had served up. I got the sense that my reactivity, and my overall stress, had reduced, which allowed me to focus on the task at hand.

For most people, stress seems to build up during the day, from the moment you wake to the moment your head hits the pillow. This accumulation of stress impairs our cognitive ability to make good decisions and be an effective leader. Mindfulness allows us to take regular 'reset moments' throughout the day to stop (and even lower) the rising stress levels before they get out of hand.

Here are some of the other reasons mindfulness helps our leadership capability.

It gives you better control over your emotions. The more we practice mindfulness and become more self-aware of how we are feeling, the more likely we are to notice when feelings and emotions arise. We notice the subtle (or not so subtle) way our body feels when something isn't quite right. By noticing this we are able to self-regulate before we react.

It improves relationships. If you are calmer, less stressed, and have better control over your emotions, it goes without saying that this also has a positive impact on relationships. I haven't met many leaders who don't have a lot of contact with people, so relationships are key to our success and the success of our team.

It makes you enjoy the experience more. Whether you are sitting in a meeting, or punching out a hard task on your computer, mindfulness is about fully experiencing whatever it is you are doing in the present moment. Instead of wishing we were somewhere else or distracting ourselves with social media, we are present and focused on the task at hand.

It makes you more grateful. When was the last time you sat down and really thought about all the things you are grateful for about your job? As humans we have a negativity bias, which means we are programmed to focus on the bad stuff in lieu of what's going well. The good news is, because of neuroplasticity, we know we can reprogram the mind to pay more attention to the good stuff as well. It just takes a bit of effort to rewire those neurons. You can be grateful for so many things: the salary, the people you work with, the flexibility, the benefits, the sense of purpose, the fact you even have a job . . . The list goes on!

It helps you sleep better. I have had countless people tell me over the years how they meditate right before sleep and how this relaxes them and allows them to transition from a hectic day into a restful slumber. As leaders we tend to carry things from our day into the bedroom, leaving us lying awake at three o'clock in the morning trying to solve the latest crisis. As mindful leaders, we are better equipped to leave a bad day at the office so we can be more present with our families and loved ones.

It makes us more focused. By practicing mindfulness, we are training our minds to more readily recognise when our attention has wandered, and to be better equipped to bring it back to the task at hand. Have you ever been reading an email or a document and you get to the end of the page and think to yourself, 'I have no idea what I just read'. You start again from the top but get the same result. You just can't seem to focus. Or, have you ever found yourself daydreaming in a meeting when all of a sudden someone ends a question with your name?

Mindfulness helps you catch yourself in the act so you can bring your attention back to where it needs to be. As a leader, wouldn't you want all these benefits?

4

Cutting Through The Myths

Whenever I teach mindful leadership to a new group, it's really interesting to see the different reactions I get from the participants. I often see their faces change almost immediately and it's usually one of three reactions. The first is a knowing look, or a nod or smile of someone who has practiced or experienced mindfulness before. The second is a look of fear like, 'Whoa I didn't sign up for this!' And finally, it may be a look of confusion that says, 'What the heck is this guy talking about?'

Today there aren't a lot of people who haven't heard about mindfulness, but every now and again it does happen. Sometimes people who have had experience with mindfulness just didn't really know what to call it.

So what is it that causes this second group of people to show a visible sign of fear, even among the strongest of our future leaders? In my experience, it is a misconception about what mindfulness actually is. Some people seem to think to be mindful you have to meditate in silence for four hours a day, wear long robes and join a monastery. In fact, I even had one gentleman ask me in a workshop once, 'Don't you have to be a monk to be mindful?'

After an initial session on mindful leadership, most of the class can see the benefits and want to commit to being more mindful in their workplaces. But every now and then, there is someone who still isn't quite sure, mainly because they have other misconceptions about what mindful is and isn't.

So I started to compile a list of myths that I have heard over the years, which I thought might be useful to dig into a little:

You have to be religious to practice mindfulness. Although it is said to have its roots in a number of ancient religions, mindfulness is not tied to any religion, nor do you have to be religious to practice. Mindfulness does not require any religious books, studies, talismans or beliefs; it is simply being present in the moment-whatever that looks like for you.

Mindfulness is trying to blank the mind. The mind is built to think and we are constantly having any number of thoughts, consciously or sub-consciously. The aim of mindfulness is not to blank the mind but to direct our focus to the present moment by bringing our attention to our breath or a single object (like a candle's flame, for example). Another common method is to just watch the thoughts, to allow them to come and go without getting caught up in them.

One of the best analogies I have heard to describe this is to imagine yourself sitting at a train station watching trains pull into and out of the station. The aim is not to get onto any of the trains but just watch them come in and go out. Trains come in. Trains go out. Our aim is to stay on that platform and not get on one of the trains. The problem with these trains (thoughts) is you never really know where you are going to end up.

Mindfulness is a relaxation technique. Well, sort of . . . Our intention when being more mindful should never be to try and become more relaxed. When you are striving to relax, if something goes wrong (or just different to the way you planned it), you will either get frustrated, or you will try even harder. Striving to achieve something that is just out of reach doesn't feel very relaxing at all. Having said that, relaxation is often a by-product of mindfulness, so let go of your expectations and just be.

Mindfulness will make me weak. On the contrary, by practicing mindfulness you are actually strengthening the brain so you have greater control over your thoughts and emotions. Mindfulness is like going to the gym for the mind. The more times you catch your mind wandering and refocus, the stronger you get. In fact, a lot of top athletes, sports teams, military leaders, hardened police officers, and even top executives use mindfulness to help them become more focused and perform at their peak.

Mindfulness is a fad. Although there has been a spike in interest in mindfulness, particularly in the last decade or so, it's not something that has just risen up out of the shadows overnight. Mindfulness has been around for centuries and will be around for centuries to come. When people practice mindfulness, they begin to appreciate that the concepts are incredibly simple but of course not necessarily easy. However, they soon find that the effort in harnessing the mind is worth the peace they experience when living more mindfully.

There are other myths out there but these tend to be the ones I hear the most. If you think of any more, or are still unsure, then by all means reach out to me because I'm always happy to clear these up.

II

Why

The importance of mindful leadership

5

Collaborative Leadership

Gone are the days of the iconic leader, the saviour, who knows everything and can solve any problem. In this age of information, we don't look to leaders to have all the answers (that's why we have Google on our phones, right?). We look to leaders to bring people who may have different experiences and talents together to come up with better answers.

A mindful leader in the twenty-first century knows the importance of working with others to get the best results. Through self-awareness they can see their own strengths and weaknesses and are happy to ask people for help where they may need it. Mindful leaders know they don't have all the answers, yet they are comfortable enough with themselves to let others see that too.

Having the ability to put your ego aside, to collaborate with the people at all levels of an organisation, is a skill required to be successful in the modern workforce. Hierarchy doesn't matter when you put the needs of the many before the needs of the self. We need to remember that everyone brings value to the team no matter where they sit on the organisation chart. And often a mindful leader can see strengths and value that other people may not even see in themselves.

I remember the first time I consciously put my ego aside when I knew I didn't have the knowledge to solve a particularly difficult problem. It felt unbelievably uncomfortable. I had the misguided and antiquated notation that I needed to be the one to answer all the problems. But I knew in this case I didn't have it. The thing that held me from bringing it to my team was the thought I would lose face with my peers or subordinates, or maybe even lose control or respect of the team. I thought if I showed I didn't have all the answers people would see it as a sign of weakness. A sense of order would be replaced by chaos as the team felt its leader was no longer capable of leading the team. It was such an eye-opening experience about my own thoughts and beliefs about leadership.

But as it turned out, I was worried for no reason. People actually started to feel more comfortable coming to me with suggestions or offering up solutions. Rather than seeing me as weak-which was my initial fear-they saw me as approachable and perhaps even more human. They started to have more buy in when issues arose as I relinquished some of the control and allowed them to take on more. This opened so many doors for us as a team, which would have never been as likely had I not let myself be so vulnerable.

I know this won't be easy for some, particularly if you have always led from the front. But we have a responsibility to the next generation of leaders to model a more inclusive behaviour. We have to show those around us that the role of the leader is to bring people together and it really doesn't matter who comes up with the answers or who gets the credit.

Successful leaders in the twenty-first century won't be the ones with all the answers. They will be the ones who can unite people and bring together every scrap of talent within their network to drive their teams forward to success. How comfortable are you with allowing others to take the leadership reins?

6

Self-Awareness

M indfulness is being aware of what is happening around you in the present moment but, perhaps more importantly, what is also happening within you. We can't do much about our thoughts, emotions, and our actions unless we truly understand where they are coming from and what is driving them.

Daniel Goleman, who literally wrote the book, *Emotional Intelligence*, says that self-awareness is the keystone of emotional intelligence[3].

Self-awareness for me is the most important component of emotional intelligence. Without the foundation of self-awareness, we can't do much about the other aspects of emotional intelligence. If we aren't self-aware, we're not as conscious of our own thoughts and emotions, or the impact that may cause on the people around us.

When we are aware of our thoughts we can choose which ones

deserve our attention and which ones do not. When those thoughts are negative they can drive us to feel unhappy, angry, or even annoyed at the people around us. When we are aware of those emotions, even though we may not be aware of the thoughts that started it, we can still refocus the mind so we don't get caught up in them.

As a mindful leader, you should have a practical awareness of your emotional intelligence strengths and limitations. It's important not to overestimate your strengths or underestimate your limitations. With this knowledge, you can better use those strengths to your advantage and minimise the potential limitations-because when we are aware of our limitations we can do something about them.

On the other hand, if we are unaware of our limitations it's likely that we are constantly falling short of our objectives, without understanding why. This is what is commonly referred to as a blind spot.

The good news is that self-awareness can absolutely be developed, and mindfulness is one of the ways we can do that. When we become more curious about what's happening in our internal life, we can start to see the impact that has on our external lives.

On a micro level, one of the best ways I find to do this is to spend time in quiet reflection. I have more 'light bulb' moments in my own life when I give myself the space to examine my thoughts and to try and uncover why I may be reacting to external triggers. I use this technique when thinking about the big things in my life: relationships, career, my leadership.

On a macro level, checking in regularly throughout my day to notice how I'm feeling and whether my thoughts are contributing to those feelings can be quite useful. By checking in, I notice how my own moods affect my actions and what impact that may be having on people around me. We should never underestimate the impact a bad mood can have on our team.

I often try and do this when I notice I've become too focused on a task. I'll stop and just notice how am I feeling right now? What is my level of stress? Am I holding onto any tension in my body? I'll also stop and notice my breath. This whole process can be as quick as thirty seconds, but it has a huge impact on my day. I also use a couple of other techniques to help me with this which we will discuss in the 'how to' section of this book.

It's important to remember that thoughts are just pre-programmed responses to stimuli. Thoughts in most cases aren't unique, they are just the way our brains process information. We are not our thoughts. We are the observer of our thoughts. Those thoughts are just our brain's way of coping with the world. But the more we believe our own thoughts and allow ourselves to get carried away by our monkey mind the more we are reinforcing the habit.

So, how do we become more aware of our monkey mind and not let it take over our reality? Let's find out in the next chapter!

7

Taming the Monkey Mind

We all have a voice in our head that sounds like someone is constantly narrating our lives-think Kevin Arnold from *The Wonder Years*(if you are old enough to know the reference). If you are sitting there thinking 'this guy is crazy, there is no voice in my head', that's the voice I'm talking about! This voice is often referred to as the 'monkey mind'.

It's so aptly named for a number of reasons but primarily because of its flighty nature, its ability to be distracted by shiny objects (or food), and the fact that it's always screeching about something.

Our monkey mind is operating twenty-four seven so it tends to fade into the background and we don't realize half the time that it's driving our thoughts and emotions. But, whether we're running through to-do lists, judging people we see on the street, or thinking about what we are going to eat for our next meal, it is always there.

During times of stress or inner turmoil the monkey mind goes into overdrive-thinking things through, analysing situations, replaying conversations, going over the same situation over and over again to try and make sense of things. It can be relentless as it flits from one thought to the next. I like to imagine my monkey mind sitting on a couch watching the commercials on TV, but in super fast forward. *Nappies. Pizza. Walking on a beach. Work got you down? Soft drink. Steak Knives.But wait, there's more!* Oh yes, my mind is a very interesting place to live.

Unless we are conscious of our monkey mind and the games it plays, these interactions can actually have quite an effect on our emotions and our mood.

One of my most destructive habits from years gone by was rehearsing conversations before they even happened. I would play the conversation out in my head, thinking about what my colleague would say, how I would react, what my comeback might be, the indignation, the under-appreciation and so on, until things would spiral out of control and I would be furious at the person without either of us having spoken a word.

Has that ever happened to you?

This process can somehow be quite addictive and a difficult habit to break. There is a sense of self-righteousness when we tell someone off in our pre-rehearsed conversation, and that can feel (falsely, of course) rather empowering.

But unfortunately those conversations are doing more harm than good. Particularly when, the next time we meet with said colleague, we launch into a tirade they never even saw coming! They usually have a look of shock on their face as they try and catch up to where you are in the conversation. This is not a great way to win friends and influence people.

There is a great quote by Mark Twain, 'I have been through some terrible things in my life, some of which actually happened'. This really sums up the whole idea of this chapter for me. If we allow our monkey mind to take control, it has a habit of creating stories or an opinion about whatever is actually happening.

Being mindful of your stories is about noticing when the voice in your head starts to spiral out of control. It's bringing yourself back to the present moment by stopping yourself from engaging those thoughts. In the first instance you may want to try the STOP technique (see: Chapter Twenty-Two: Time to STOP) or just come back to the basics and focus on three slow, mindful breaths.

It's funny, our minds often can't tell the difference between internal interactions (or things that happen to us in our minds) or real-life interactions (things that *actually* happen). They basically feel the same because both stir emotions within us. So whether we are walking around having real negative interactions, or we are just telling ourselves negative stories about that same person, in both cases we are adding to the lens in which we actually see the person. And this can have massive repercussions in our relationships both at work and at home.

8

Thriving on Busy

Some people get a real rush from being busy! Struggling to meet multiple deadlines, multi-tasking, running from one meeting to the next-it can actually be exhilarating for some people. The heightened state of stress causes adrenaline to rush through our bodies, which can feel like a natural high. But if, deep down, we know that not allowing ourselves time to rest and recover can be dangerous for our physical and mental health, why do we do it? Some people thrive on busy because of the rush, but others put themselves through it because of the culture we create in our workplaces.

When I conduct leadership programs, I often ask participants what their biggest issues with time management are. I will ask them a series of questions, one of which is whether they thrive on being busy. Invariably the majority of the participants in the room will put up their hand acknowledging that this is something they struggle with.

Why should the majority of people feel like they want to (or have to) work at such a frenetic pace despite knowing the potential side effects? Is it the social status of saying how busy we are? Or could it be the sense of importance we associate with being busy that we are trying to achieve? Or are people afraid that if they say they are managing their workload okay, that the boss will just give them more work to do?

It's great to be busy and get things done, but at what cost? When is too much, too much?

Just because you are a mindful leader doesn't mean you won't get busy. The difference is that a mindful leader will take time out during their day to pause and to check in with themselves and those around them, despite their workload. And they will do it without the additional layer of storytelling that often comes with being busy-why me? How will I get all this done? This can have a significant impact on how stressed they feel at the end of the day.

If you are in a constant state of stress for eight, ten, or even twelve hours a day, it can have a cumulative effect. Now, what if that occurs five, six or seven days a week? Our bodies aren't designed to manage that amount of stress over such a long period of time.

It's important to know that as humans our productivity starts to decline the longer we work. Multiple studies have proven that the mind can only go so hard for so long before it starts to lose focus and becomes unproductive. It's different for everyone, however the accepted norm for focused attention is somewhere between forty-five to ninety minutes[4]. That's about as far as we can work at our optimal level before the wheels might start coming off.

This is why taking regular breaks throughout our day-and I mean a proper break, not just pushing back from your desktop computer so you can scroll through your phone-is imperative for us to perform at our best.

As a leader, people look to us to set the standard. If we are thriving on being busy and not proactively showing positive ways of managing our workload throughout our day, how can we expect our people to feel comfortable to do the same? And when we reward others for working late or pushing through their lunch break, we are sending a very strong message to the people around us about what we value. What we do has a ripple effect throughout our team and, ultimately, throughout the organisation we work for.

We need to redefine what success looks like for us and for our teams. Are we promoting a culture where people who are overwhelmed with busyness and working crazy hours are the standard? Or should we create a culture of wholeness, where we look after one another and ourselves so together we can achieve great things-but not at the expense of our mental or physical health.

It's time to start making sure we take regular breaks throughout the day to pause and be mindful. The techniques in Part Two of this book will help you do just that.

9

Avoiding Burnout

Whether we are thriving on busy or can't control the level of stress in our jobs, if we spend too long in this state of heightened stress it can ultimately lead to burnout.

Burnout can show up in a number of different ways depending on people's circumstances but includes the following:

- frustration or irritability
- cynicism or disillusionment
- disengagement
- lack of energy, drive, or motivation
- prolonged periods of unproductivity or inefficiency (slipping job performance)
- increase in headaches, migraines, or tension headaches
- lack of self-care (over/under-eating, lack of personal hygiene, etc)
- depression

As a leader we need to be finely attuned to what is happening with our team but also within ourselves. If you notice any prolonged periods of the above signs, or a dramatic change in yours or others' behaviour, it's time to assess what's happening underneath.

What are the stressors that are contributing to the feeling of burnout? Has it been a period of heightened activity or a time when there has been a lot of change in your organisation (we will talk about change fatigue in Chapter Fifteen: Leading Change). Is this something that will naturally die down after a major project ends, for example, or do you need to intervene? Either way this is something that needs to be addressed.

It's then important to put in an action plan for how you will address this issue going forward. What needs to change? What are your options? Is this really the job for you? Does it match your core values? As Don Schlitz wrote in the song 'The Gambler', 'You got to know when to hold 'em, know when to fold 'em'.

After doing the above self-reflection, you may find a change of perspective is required. Sometimes coming at the same problem from a different angle gives you the different perspective you need to see what's really going on. How can you make your work more enjoyable? Are you taking enough time for you during the day to reset your stress levels? Do you need to increase your mindfulness practices? I could write my whole next book on why work shouldn't have to suck and what you can do about it!

Something that is often overlooked when you are overwhelmed with busyness is the value of exercise in regulating stress. It's hard to find time to exercise when we are so busy, but exercise is invaluable in keeping your mind and your body functioning at optimal levels. If you stop exercising it contributes to the physical symptoms of stress but also the mental ones as well. So make sure you keep up your physical activity because I guarantee you it's going to help.

The last thing I want to say in this chapter is to make sure you get help when it's needed. You don't need to suffer in silence. If you are feeling overwhelmed or close to burnout (check the list again) make sure you speak up. Sometimes people around you won't act because they can't tell that anything is wrong. Whether it's your co-workers, manager, friends, or loved ones, there is no shame in asking for help.

10

Reducing Stress in the Workplace

As leaders we have a lot of information constantly going around in our heads. So much so that it can feel like there is no more room to fit anything in! We think about things that have happened in the past, tasks we have been given, things we have agreed to do, or even things that have gone wrong. Or we are focused on what's happening in the future: looming deadlines, upcoming presentations, or difficult situations we may have to manage. With all of these things going around in our heads there's little wonder that stress in the workplace is on the rise.

One of our key responsibilities as leaders in any workplace is monitoring and managing workplace stress. There are so many different factors contributing to stress in the workplace-long hours, heavy workload, tight deadlines, poor leadership, change, and the list goes on. The rise of stress in the workplace is the reason the World Health Organization has dubbed it the 'health epidemic of the twenty-first century[5]'.

As leaders, we have a responsibility to our organisations to ensure our teams are productive and running as efficiently as possible. Our role is to ensure the never-ending cycle of tasks and projects are completed on time and on budget. However, if we focus purely on output it can be to the detriment of our greatest asset-our people! There needs to be a balance of completing tasks and monitoring those around us for signs of stress and fatigue. As leaders, we need to ensure that we are not only looking after our own mental wellbeing, but also for those we lead.

A mindful leader is someone who manages stress within themselves and others to produce optimal outcomes for their team and their organisation. They are better able to self-regulate their emotions and the emotions of those around them. This enables them to make better decisions in an increasingly complex and challenging work environment. There is so much research available online nowadays that proves how mindfulness reduces stress levels[6], lowers blood pressure[7], and can restore a sense of wellbeing[8].

Incorporating mindfulness into your leadership practice en-ables you to become more aware of what is happening in your world, both internally and externally. It involves 'checking in' regularly throughout your day to notice any stress or negative feelings that may be creeping in or taking over. We use those signals to let us know how we are travelling and whether now may be the time to take a moment to focus on bringing the stress levels down.

When you notice you're feeling stressed it gives you the power to choose what comes next. Do you keep pushing through to make sure you can check another thing off the list, or do you take a moment to just breathe and try to re-centre yourself? So often we choose to ignore the sense of unease or the feelings of stress because we are either too busy to notice or it feels like we have no other option than to just keep going.

11

Put on Your Oxygen Mask First

If you have ever flown in an aircraft before I'm sure you will know the meaning behind this chapter's title before I even explain it. But in case you have never been on a plane, or have slept through all of the safety briefings (you know who you are!), you probably can still see where I'm going to go with this.

Before we can help others we have to help ourselves first-because if we are in a state of stress or suffering, we are less likely to be able to help others when they are feeling stressed or going through difficult times.

Leaders have a drive and passion to serve others, but sometimes that can come at the expense of their own health. 'Oh, John, you're having a tough week and can't finish that report? I'll do it mate', or, 'Suzy, don't worry about that last task, you head on home to your family-I got this'. And then, all of a sudden, what was a full workload is suddenly bursting at the seams and you are the one left to carry the load.

I'm not saying we shouldn't be putting others before ourselves, and I'm certainly not saying we shouldn't help others in need. But we do need to recognise our own limitations as a human being and the toll it takes when our own stress levels start to get out of control. To be in the best place to help others, we need to put on our own oxygen masks first.

There is often reluctance by leaders to ask for help when the load gets too heavy. We seem to think we can battle on if we just push a little harder for a little longer. Putting our hands up for help should never be seen as a sign of weakness or failure as a leader. It's a sign of strength to be able to recognise that you are at a stretch point and need to release the tension so you don't snap like a rubber band.

If we are going to be effective as leaders, and serve others to the best of our ability, we have to look after our own mental health as a priority. It's not enough to notice when others are suffering or going through hard times, we have to notice when it's happening to ourselves.

Often as leaders we think we aren't susceptible to stress, or we can just push through until the weekend. The problem is that cumulative stress will eventually catch us, and unfortunately sometimes when we least expect it.

We need to be constantly vigilant and take proactive measures to ensure the right balance between productivity and maintenance. As most car owners would know, to get the most mileage out of a car we need to do a few things to keep the car running: we need to add fuel, we need to ensure the tyres are inflated and have enough tread, we need to ensure the engine is regularly maintained and is running efficiently.

What happens if we fail to do these things? We run out of gas. We blow a tyre. Or the car breaks down on the side of the road and we are left with a massive repair bill and no ability to get from A to B.

Our mental health is just like that car. We need to ensure we are maintaining our minds regularly if we want to get the best mileage and be at our most productive. But the stakes are much higher when it comes to mental health, because if we have a break down it's not as simple as swapping out the engine.

We need to model the behaviour we expect to see in others and create the conditions for wellness in the workplace. Too often, people want to be more mindful in the workplace but the culture doesn't allow it. As leaders, the standard we set for our teams-and ourselves-is often the first step in creating a new culture.

Often we don't feel comfortable about doing something different or challenging the status quo. But that's leadership. And I can think of no better reason to break the cultural norm than looking after people's mental wellbeing in the workplace.

What standard are you setting in your workplace?

12

What Are Your Emotional Triggers?

I n life there are always going to be certain things that bother you more than others. Whenever these things occur—we call them triggers—they are more than likely going to cause a reaction within you. This initial, internal reaction can often lead to an external, outward reaction. These reactions can be small or really big depending on our circumstances and how we are feeling at the time. They manifest in a range of ways but can include signs of aggression, anger, stress, sadness, or a range of other negative emotions.

We call them triggers because it feels like it's an automatic reaction that we have little control over. Something happens and it causes a reaction. If you think of the analogy of someone firing a gun, as soon as you pull the trigger, the gun fires a split second later. The gun doesn't think about it, it doesn't try and reason with the internal mechanisms that cause the bullet to be propelled towards its target. It just happens.

Some people don't think they have a choice when something

triggers an emotional reaction. They think the automatic response is just 'who they are' or justify their behaviour by explaining what caused the reaction in the first place. But we do have a choice! There is a moment between when the trigger is pulled, and when our reaction fires, where we get to make a choice.

There is a quote I love (and refer to often) by Viktor Frankl that says, 'Between stimulus and response there is a space. In that space is our power to choose our response. In our response lies our growth and our freedom'. Frankl was a holocaust survivor who was interned in the Nazi prison camps during World War II. He wrote about the atrocities he saw and experienced as a captive. If someone like Viktor can remain mindful in situations like these, I think we can all learn to be a little more mindful in our daily lives.

To gain more control over our triggers, we first have to learn what our triggers are and how they occur. Some of you may have a good idea of what your triggers are already and can probably list a number of them without too much thought. If you can't, it may be worthwhile reflecting on the last couple of times you felt angry or upset and think about what was at the root of your reaction. It can be helpful to write these reflections down to help you keep track.

Often our triggers may be at the subconscious level, so we can't easily put our finger on what's causing the issue. We either misdiagnose the trigger or get it wrong altogether. Sometimes we have to go a little deeper to figure out what's really wrong. It's not always the tip of the iceberg that's the trouble; it's the rest of the unseen ice hidden under the water.

If you are struggling to come up with a list, another way of uncovering your triggers is to keep a journal for the next week of things that cause a reaction within you. At the end of each day (or as each trigger is set off, if that's easy enough) write down what the trigger was, what emotion you experienced, and, on a scale of one to ten, the strength of your reaction.

Once we have learned what our triggers are we can then think about putting together an action plan to figure out how we may be better able to respond in those situations, rather than react. Let me give you an example:

Betty is an introvert who likes to start work early so she can get her work done without disruptions. She loves the quiet as she can focus on her tasks without people interrupting her and she gets a lot done. David is an extrovert who rocks up to work a little later than others but always has time for a chat. He's a people person and loves engaging with his colleagues on a social level as well as a professional one.

Every morning David arrives, Betty can feel herself getting annoyed even before David says good morning. She thinks to herself, 'Why does he have to interrupt me, can't he see I'm working?' This causes a negative reaction within Betty that sees her grunt a greeting on her best days and snap David's head off on her worst.

After attending some mindfulness training, Betty realises that David's interruptions are triggering a negative reaction within her. She decides that it is unproductive to feel this way and these feelings are unnecessary.

When David arrives at work, this time Betty takes a pause from her tasks and allows herself to breathe and just be present. She uses the feeling of unease rising within her to remind her to choose a different response. Rather than worrying about the loss of productivity, she realises that this mindful minute is a way of connecting with her colleague and not allowing stress to creep into her day. When David says good morning she greets him with a cheerful hello and even asks how he is.

Not every day is easy for Betty, particularly when she is stressed or facing a tight deadline. But the more she practices, the easier it becomes. Pretty soon it's just part of Betty's normal daily routine.

The great thing about our minds is that they can be programmed for different responses. If our reactions to date don't serve us, maybe it's time to choose a different way of responding to things. The more we practice our responses, the more automated they become until the neural pathways are so strong we can't believe we ever responded any differently.

For some people this can be a fairly easy task; it takes some time and practice but eventually it just works. For others, they need to dig a little deeper. Unfortunately when change doesn't come quickly, I've seen that often they just give up. I would suggest doing a little more research on the power of habits and learn how you can more effectively apply this in your life (see: Reading List). Despite what the old saying says, you can teach an old dog new tricks!

What are your triggers and how do they show up for you? What can you put in place to make sure you are responding to a situation rather than reacting?

13

Time to Respond

Have you ever found yourself reacting badly in a situation, which you later regretted? This may have happened because you were under pressure: someone wanted a response straight away, or maybe there were heightened emotions because of a conflict or stressful situation. Do you remember why you chose to react in that moment?

I know from my own experience that my first reaction in a situation is often wrong. I can get caught up in my emotions, overreact, be biased in my response, and even limit my choices because I don't see all the options available to me.

When stressed, we actually have less mental capacity to skilfully respond to a situation than when we are in a calmer state. At the time when we need our cognitive abilities more than ever, the brain abandons us to deal with the extra bodily functions caused by our stressed state. This reduces the overall capacity of the brain and our capability to deal with the situation effectively.

Often as leaders we feel obliged to respond to a situation straight away because 'that's what leaders do'. You've asked a question, so now I must give you my answer straight away. There is a crisis; people are looking at me to lead so I had better start doing something now. But this is a fool's errand. If we know we have less mental capacity, why do we choose to give our response immediately when we know we aren't in the best frame of mind?

One of my colleagues I worked with many years ago took a different approach that really resonated with me. He was an incident command and control systems expert; these are the police officers who turn up to major emergency situations, take command of the scene, and coordinate the response. Imagine the adrenaline and the stress these police officers must be under when they first turn up to these emergency situations.

He taught police officers that whenever they turned up to a scene, the first thing they should do is put their hands in their pockets and take a breath. Yes, you read that correctly. He taught them to fight their natural instincts to jump straight in and start solving problems so that they could allow themselves time to manage their own emotional state first. This gives them time to naturally reduce their stress levels and increase their mental capacity to deal with the situation at hand. This whole process may only take thirty seconds, but that is enough time to better mentally prepare themselves to deal with the situation effectively.

What's stopping you from giving yourself thirty seconds? Or, if it's not a life or death situation, thirty minutes to prepare yourself to respond more effectively? I usually find that if I tell my team to let me 'ponder that for a minute', they completely understand and give me that time. In most situations that's enough time for me to just notice the affect the stress is having on my body and allow me to take a few deep breaths. Under stress our breathing pattern is affected and it becomes shorter and shallower. Consciously taking deeper breaths allows us to reverse some of the impacts of the stress and that in turn gives us more mental capacity to deal with the situation.

If that's not enough time, I take a walk around the block. The combination of movement, getting outside for some fresh air and a little space from the situation gives me a whole new perspective. Automatically I feel calmer from the exercise as the blood starts to work its way around my body. But it also gives me time to run through the decision more comprehensively, helping me to make sure I have covered all of the bases.

The next time one of your team comes to you with a problem, just notice if this interaction is causing you to feel stressed. If it is, ask yourself, 'Can I give myself some time here to properly formulate a response so I won't regret my knee-jerk reaction later?' And if you can give yourself a little time-do it! Give it a try; see how much more effective you can be if you just allow yourself some time and space before you respond.

14

Remaining Mindful During Conflict

As leaders, we may have to face conflict on a regular basis, no matter how easygoing we think we may be. Many things have the potential to lead to conflict—difficult conversations, saying no to someone, asking someone for something, difficult people, the list goes on. The question is, how do you remain mindful during conflict so you can thoughtfully engage in the conversation and get the right outcome for you and your team?

Evolution has basically equipped us with three options when it comes to conflict: fight, flight, or freeze. So when faced with conflict, our body automatically starts preparing us physiologically to either engage our enemy or run for the hills. Blood begins to head towards our limbs and large muscle groups so we are ready to run (leg muscles) or fight (chest, arms and legs). Adrenaline and cortisol flood our body. Our heart starts racing and palms begin to sweat. Our breathing rate increases.

This may have been useful in the days of the dinosaurs, we really only needed those three options, but in a modern world there aren't too many prehistoric predators roaming our urban streets. There is actually a fourth option—use our heads. Unfortunately we haven't yet evolved enough as a species to get a physiological response of increased brain function during times of stress. So at the time when you really need your brain to function at its peak, you can barely string two sentences together because your body is busily preparing you for good old fight, flight, or freeze.

Using mindfulness during conflict allows us to override our body's natural responses so we can remain calm and focused. By being more mindful during conflict, we are heightening our sense of consciousness to a point where we can start to become more aware of the present moment, our thoughts, and our emotions.

The first step is to notice when the conflict starts heading down an unproductive behaviour track and to be aware that you need to stop that train as quickly as possible. For some people this is done by noting and measuring their physiological response: the breath, the racing heart, or the feeling of anxiety. For others, it's recognising the voice in their head that says, 'Oh no, this isn't going well'. We need to fight our primal urges to release the emotional floodgates and move away from unproductive communication in the form of yelling, insults, and aggressive behaviour.

If you're aware it's time to change, give yourself a pat on the back—that can be half the battle! Now just try taking a few deep, calming breaths. This will help you regulate most of the physiological responses and get you out of the fight, flight, or freeze mode. Stay present in the conversation, but at the same time just keep slowing your breath until you start to feel a little calmer.

Our overall goal in these situations should be to respond, not react; however, this is difficult if we are not able to regulate our thoughts and emotions. Remember from the last chapter that we get to choose whether we react or respond, but we have to train our mind to get the best outcomes.

In conflict situations, our subjective mind often takes over, pulling us into story mode. As discussed in Chapter Six: Taming the Monkey mind, our brains like to make up stories so we can make better sense of what is happening in our world. The problem with these stories is they are often one-sided and inflammatory. At this point, ask yourself a couple of key clarifying questions:

- What is your intention for this argument? Is it to be right? Or is there a bigger picture? How important is this working relationship to you?
- Will this matter a year from now? Often when we are in the heat of battle we can't see the forest for the trees. Taking a longer view can often give us the perspective we need to recognise whether or not this is that important in the big scheme of things.
- How would this look from the other person's perspective? How have you contributed to this conflict? Stephen Covey says we need to, 'Seek first to understand, then to be

understood[9]'. Use your active listening skills to find out what is really at the heart of the issue for the other person (hint: sometimes it's not just the words they are saying).

- What is the right thing to do? This powerful question should give you clarification on whether you back down or stand your ground. You need to choose your battles—but do it for the right reason.

At this point, it might be useful to think of this conflict as an opportunity for you to practice your communication skills. That subtle mindset shift can often be enough to redirect your energy away from anger and towards the challenge of communicating more thoughtfully. When we are focusing on improving ourselves, our agenda changes from the one we may have had when the conflict started to get off track.

You now have the tools to go out and practise being more mindful during conflict. However, just because you may start practising this new style of communication today, doesn't necessarily mean you are going to become an expert overnight. It's a muscle that needs to be exercised regularly if you really want to improve your ability to be more mindful during conflict. So remember, practice makes perfect.

15

Technology Takeover

L et me start this chapter by confessing, I am a bit of a tech geek. I have a phone, a tablet, a smart watch, an e-book reader, a laptop—okay, I think I will leave that list right there! As a writer, a digital training consultant, an employee, a leader and entrepreneur, I can always find a good reason why my tech should never be too far away.

With our easy access to technology devices—and the number of different platforms through which we receive information—we seem to be online from the moment we wake up until the moment we switch out the light (and probably a little bit after that for some of us!). One recent study by Asurion discovered that users were checking their smartphones over eighty times a day[10]. Apple has confirmed this startling figure, saying the average user of the iPhone unlocks their device eighty times a day[11]. Why do we do it? We get a small dopamine hit every time we check our phone, and the designers of apps and social media know it. That is why they have specifically designed these platforms to leave us wanting more.

In the workplace, things aren't any better. We often work at computers, take notes on our tablets, and talk to clients or colleagues on our smartphones. Then, when it's time for a break, we set aside our computers so we can look at our smartphones—then we go straight back to our computers. It's hardly a break at all!

How are we meant to relax if we don't take a break from the relentless mental stimulation? The unending input from multiple platforms on multiple devices can lead to information overload. Yet rather than taking a technology break, it becomes like a drug that we constantly need access to and need bigger doses of to satisfy our urges.

The craving and need for more information can end up feeling like a mild case of attention deficit hyperactivity disorder (ADHD). You feel a sense of hyper vigilance as you wait for the next ping, beep, like, or tweet. If there were ever a business case for mindful leadership, this alone would suffice.

As a leader, you have a responsibility to ensure technology is used responsibly in the workplace. What is your company (or your own) policy on using personal devices during business hours? How do you monitor usage and who enforces the standards? This may seem rather draconian, however, for the latest generation who are entering the workplace, no one has ever told them it's not okay to be on their personal device all day.

Often people pretend not to notice because it's too hard to enforce or they don't want to be 'that person'. As a leader it's important to have the conversation early, particularly if there are clearly defined rules around use of technology that are being ignored.

How do you model the behaviours you expect to see in your team? What does it tell them if you are the one constantly stopping to check your phone even when people are trying to talk to you? As a mindful leader, you need to set the standard you want to see in others.

How often do you encourage your team to step away from their devices and take a 'real' break? The challenge of leading teams nowadays often extends across borders and even across nations. We cannot expect that our teams will always be located in the same country, let alone under the same roof. The use of technology in these cases is paramount to our success; however, as we are becoming a more mobile and integrated workforce, the line between home and work is becoming blurred.

What is your policy on work devices in the home? How available do you make yourself out of hours for your team and for your clients?

It may feel like there are more questions than answers in this chapter, however I am conscious of that fact that every situation is different. The role of a mindful leader is to reflect on their own situation and find a solution that best suits their needs.

Something I personally try and do every day is to take a mini tech vacation (notice I said mini vacation there; I think some people would have felt very nervous at the prospect of being away from their devices for too long!). I step away from all devices for up to two hours and don't go near them unless it's an emergency. If I need to make a note or put something in my calendar I will get out an old-fashioned pen and paper and write it down so I don't forget when the self-imposed embargo has ended.

The other thing I try and do is positively use technology to ensure I am being more mindful. There are literally hundreds of apps out there designed to help you be more present, practice mindfulness, or even meditate. You can set a reminder on your phone to be mindful at set points throughout the day. I have notifications on my smart watch that remind me during the day to be more mindful or just breathe for one minute.

The differences these tips make on my day are significant. I encourage those around me to also try these methods, particularly if I notice someone hasn't taken a break for an extended period. By using technology to be more mindful, we are trying to find a balance between usefulness and overuse.

Don't forget that technology is still overall a very positive thing. It's a choice regarding how we interact with our technology; we don't have to be a slave to the machines! As a mindful leader, encourage those around you to interact with their technology more positively. Set the standard, enforce it, and stick to it yourself.

16

Leading Change

C hange is the new constant. There is no longer a question of if things will change; it is a question of when and how things will change. Change creates uncertainty within people, which is why this has become perhaps one of our greatest leadership challenges. It is becoming more evident every day that the pace of change has increased, making it increasingly difficult to lead from a static position.

We are living in what experts are calling a VUCA world. VUCA is an acronym to describe the volatility, uncertainty, complexity, and ambiguity that is present in so many different situations and contexts. The term was first introduced by the US military but is now commonly used to describe the rapidly changing landscape of leadership and organisational change.

Organisationally, this has led to a rise in 'change fatigue' in many companies. People tend to view change as a threat, which activates our fight, flight, or freeze response. Change fatigue occurs when the constant change management processes make people feel like they are living in a state of flux for long periods of time.

Emotions aren't bad things. They are just pieces of information that tell us there are reactions occurring within our body in response to the current stimulus. As humans, we try to contextualise this information by creating a story behind why this is happening to us. As these stories are fuelled by negative thoughts and emotions, however, it can lead to people catastrophising what the outcomes might be. Left unchecked, this can lead us to believe that these stories are indeed true, and so are more than likely to come to fruition.

Reflect on the last time you experienced change in your workplace. What happened? How did you and the people around you react? Were you able to lead your team through the change with minimal disruption?

Early in my career, I found it difficult to not get caught up in the energy of change. Some of that energy was positive, looking at opportunities and ways to capitalise on what was occurring. But some of the energy was negative, uncertainty about the future and concern about potential outcomes.

It wasn't until I was in a leadership position that I became aware of how others around me were affected by my energy about the change. I began to notice that when I was excited for the change, it would have a positive impact on my team and I could see them slowly buying into the change process. Unfortunately, on reflection, my negative energy about change was also contagious.

We need to continuously adapt when leading others and ourselves in an increasingly uncertain operating environment. When mindfully leading others through change it is critical to be clear on our thoughts and emotional state before dealing with others. We must rely on our own emotional intelligence to figure out how this is affecting us and then manage how we need to regulate our behaviour in the work environment.

Sometimes we are in a position where, despite our own feelings, we just have to accept the change. If we don't get on board the 'change train' it will end up just running us down. Being mindfully aware of your thoughts and feelings in these cases can help you figure out how to work your way through the process.

When you are ready to open a dialogue with those around you about the change, it is important you start with how this will affect the individuals. You need to be very clear on what the change is and why the change is occurring. This communication should occur as early and with much information as possible.

People can feel threatened when they are dealing with uncertainty, particularly if they are left in the dark. They find it hard to focus on being productive while there is sense of the unknown hanging over their head. It's our job as leaders to make things as clear and certain as possible for them.

Don't forget that when any change occurs in the workplace,

there is going to be a reaction. Often when things change there is a sense of loss that needs to be acknowledged—and even mourned—before people can move on. This is particularly the case if it's a loss of entitlement or if people were attached to the old way of doing things.

I worked in an organisation where a large group of people lost an allowance that saw their salary decrease by about twenty percent, including mine. That was a difficult period in the organisation and it had a massive impact on morale and productivity. It was interesting to watch the different leaders during this period. Everybody dealt with the change differently, but those who were allowed to talk about it openly and work through their emotions were the ones who bounced back the quickest.

As a leader, you need to take your time to work through these issues patiently with your team. They will need emotional support and your compassion during times of change. You will need to follow up with them, on more than one occasion, and be there for them when they are ready to start working through the issues. Remember, different people have different grieving processes so it's about allowing that to naturally happen for your people in their own time.

Change takes us outside of our comfort zone, which can be a little too uncomfortable for some people. I have found people to be like rubber bands. Some rubber bands you can stretch and stretch and they seem to be able to keep growing. Other rubber bands you only have to hint at stretching them and they snap. Leaders need to know their people and know how far they can stretch them. It's not a one size fits all approach—in fact, almost every one of your people will have different stretch capability and different breaking points. You need to know how far you can stretch your people without breaking them.

There are some amazing books out there that go into more detail on the stages of change and walk you through managing and leading each stage. John P. Kotter is a respected culture change expert and has published a number of great books on this subject. I would encourage you to read them if you want a better understanding of how you can lead change in your organisation. If you are looking for a specific title, start with *Leading Change*.

The last thing I will say about dealing with change is that you must remember to breathe. During these periods of uncertainty, and while dealing with staff who are suffering from stress, it's easy to get caught up in their emotional state. Remember to put on your own oxygen mask first and breathe!

17

Building Mindful Teams

Leading and managing people can be hard work. There are lots of different things you need to give your attention to: different personalities, different needs, and sometimes even different agendas. So how do we build a more mindful team, regardless of the team's dynamics? Maintaining your own mindfulness practice can be difficult enough in the midst of a busy day with deadlines to meet and people to manage. So how do you even bring up the topic of mindfulness and then try and embed daily practices among the team?

Slowly!

I think the best way to introduce mindfulness into a team is to lead by example. Show people how you practice mindfulness in the workplace and be open to having the conversation about what it is you're doing. In some organisations there can be a real stigma in doing something as simple as stopping for a minute to focus on the breath, so it's important to let them know that it's okay to try it, and, in fact, even encouraged.

Once people have seen you practicing mindfulness, you can start to encourage them to learn more about the practice or even try mindfulness for themselves. In my experience people are often very curious about mindfulness and will have lots of questions. Nowadays most people have heard about mindfulness, however there are some who will be completely new to the subject. They may even have some misconceptions about mindfulness, so you may want to re-read Chapter Three: Cutting Through the Myths.

It's useful to build a common language around what mindfulness is and what activities are easy to do in the workplace. Breaking down the practice and dispelling any misconceptions is usually enough for some people to want to try it. If you have already started to talk about it, it then becomes easier to broach the subject of trying some group practices when the time feels right.

As you start to gain momentum, you can slowly introduce mindfulness into other normal office activities such as team scrums, formal meetings, or even lunchtime activities. Maybe it's a mindful walk around the block, or you could just sit together quietly during a coffee break. You will get the best results if you can find the activities that work best in your business environment and for your team.

Make sure you offer them the space to practice mindfulness by encouraging them to get out from behind their desks or take regular breaks throughout their day. Encourage them to not eat at their desks, but to go to the break room or eat outside if they can. By doing these little things, and encouraging others to do the same, you may be able to embed some healthier workplace practices.

Make sure you walk the talk! Lead by example and show people you are as serious about their mental health as you are about your own. People can then sense your authenticity and will appreciate your compassion for them as people. Now that's leadership!

Another way of encouraging people to be more mindful is to reflect on situations as they arise. These situations can be either positive or negative, but it's a useful way to check in with how they are feeling about the situation and how they are judging it. It may be useful to discuss these as a group or with each individual. Use these discussions to learn what people's triggers are and offer suggestions on how they may be more mindful in the future.

Some people will jump right on board the mindfulness train. I have seen some teams instantly implement mindfulness in a variety of different ways and get fantastic results. I have, on the other hand, seen other teams struggle with only half the members willing to give it a go. Often it's one or two members' unwillingness that influences the rest of the group.

It's important to remember that we never force people to take up a mindfulness practice. We don't pressure them to try it, and we certainly don't make them feel guilty if they don't want to. Mindfulness isn't for everybody and that's okay. You need to find a way to ensure people who don't want to try mindfulness don't feel excluded or left out of team activities. In most cases this involves a conversation with the person (or people) to figure out what works best for them.

As with any habit, when you are building the mindfulness practice with your team, start small and regular. Start with one mindfulness activity that takes three to five minutes at the most—something people will feel comfortable with, without being stretched too far. If you can schedule something daily that's awesome, but it may need to start a little less regularly until you gain some momentum. Use the chapters in this book as a way of prompting or guiding the conversation. Again, this is not a one-size-fits-all approach! As the leader, you are in the best position to judge what works for your team.

III

How

Strategies for embodying mindful leadership

18

Start Small

I t seems everybody I speak to likes the idea of being more mindful, or may even want to learn how to meditate, but the number one thing stopping them is time. This misconception is so common that it seems like it's almost a valid reason for people not to practice. 'Oh you don't have time to meditate, why didn't you just say so?' The problem is, the myth just isn't true.

You don't need to sit on a mountaintop for days on end practicing formal meditation to start the practice. Nor do you have to spend hours in silence or quiet contemplation to experience the benefits of mindfulness. You don't even have to go to a special room in the house to do it. It can be done anywhere and anytime, in fact, you can even do it in under a minute.

There are two avenues to start being more mindful in the workplace. One is what I like to call a micro-meditation practice. This is where you stop whatever you are doing and just breathe for a predetermined amount of time, usually a minute. The second is incorporating mindfulness into your activities, so instead of stopping to meditate, you continue doing what you were doing—just with more awareness and presence.

The micro-meditation practice is useful because it forces you to stop throughout the day and just breathe. Just stopping for a minute to focus on our breath is enough to regulate your stress levels and restore a sense of calm in your day. There is so much power in stopping whatever it is you are doing and just being present for a minute, particularly when you are really busy.

What's the best way to practice for a marathon if you've never run one before? You wouldn't turn up on race day expecting to run the full distance on your first attempt. You'd start small and slowly build your way up to the required distance over a period of time. You'd also make sure you practice regularly to help build up your endurance. It's exactly the same with meditation: you need to start small and build your way up over time. The reason I first struggled with meditation in the beginning is I found sitting for long periods of time extremely difficult.

If you have the best of intentions but often forget to pause during the day for your micro meditation, you can set an alarm on your phone or computer to remind you. In the beginning this is a really great way to start forming your mindfulness habit. Start small-once or twice a day is enough to begin with. Once you gain some momentum and feel more comfortable in your practice, you can build to whatever works best for you.

I still find it useful to set a reminder on my smart watch so I don't forget my practice, particularly as I can get engrossed in my daily activities. Having said that, the reminder always seems to happen at the worst times, whether I'm on the phone with a colleague, in the middle of a meeting, or in front of a full class of participants-you could almost set your watch by it (pun intended).

Don't worry, it's perfectly acceptable to press snooze if the timing doesn't work for you. I couldn't imagine saying halfway through a presentation, 'Sorry, guys, if you wouldn't mind just talking among yourselves for the next minute, I just need to do a quick meditation'. Wouldn't happen!

Another way of remembering your practice is to use an event to remind you to start your micro-meditation. Coffee breaks, lunch breaks, going to the bathroom, getting back from the bathroom, starting work, leaving to go home, these are all triggers you could use as a reminder to pause and take a breath. For example, when you feel the need to go to the bathroom, just pause and breathe before you stand up. When you have finished your micro-meditation, you can then go about your business.

Alternatively, there are lots of other ways to be mindful throughout your day by incorporating mindfulness into your daily activities. Finding what works for you is the key. We will explore other mindfulness suggestions in this book that you can tailor to suit your lifestyle or time demands.

At the end of the day, the only real way we can get lasting benefits from mindfulness and meditation is by building it up to a regular practice. Mindfulness is not something you can do once and then you are set for life. It's about finding a sustainable way to incorporate it into your life.

Once you start experiencing the calm and the peace that comes with micro-meditations, you'll want to start having mindful minutes throughout your day.

19

The Micro Meditation

S o what should you do during your micro meditation? Do you need to bust out your yoga mat in the middle of the office lunch room? Do you need to chant 'Om' loud and proud so everyone in the office knows what you are doing?

Don't laugh, I've had variations of these questions before. Luckily, the answer is a resounding no!

In its simplest form, the micro meditation is just stopping for sixty seconds and focusing on the breath. You don't need any equipment or a special location; you can even do it sitting at your desk. In fact, you can meditate without any one even noticing.

One of my favourite ways of 'catching my breath' at my desk (and also my secret weapon-well, until now!) is to pick a spot on the computer screen and just allow my gaze to soften. Then I just breathe. I let go of any tension in my body and I just focus on the physical sensations of my breath. I don't close my eyes or change my physical position, I just breathe.

In the five years I have been doing this, no one has ever noticed or commented (though I'm sure they will now!). For most people walking past your desk, it looks like you are just reading something on your computer. If you get interrupted, don't worry about it. Deal with the interruption and, when you are ready start the clock from the beginning, it's only sixty seconds.

While you are focusing on your breath, thoughts are going to come up. That's completely natural-in fact, I would be worried if they didn't! It's just your mind doing the thing it has become so accustomed to doing-overthinking.

Whenever a thought comes up we need to just let it go and refocus our attention on the breath. The real practice in mindfulness is not having no thoughts; it's noticing when a thought comes up and then gently bringing your attention back to the breath. It's a strengthening exercise. Every time you do it, consider it the equivalent to one bicep curl, but for your mind.

In the beginning, if you are really worried about forgetting your thoughts-particularly if you feel they are important-feel free to break from your micro meditation to write it down. Sometimes trying to focus on the breath while you are trying hard not to forget something can be a losing battle. But if you do pause, make sure you start your micro meditation from the beginning to get the full benefit.

I have found that, by doing this practice for one minute just a few times a day, I feel less stressed and more at ease at the end of even my most hectic work days. I notice a huge difference and the people around me notice the difference too.

20

Waking Up

How do you greet your day? What is the first thing you do when you wake up? Do you roll over and grab your phone, flicking through the news and social media sites to see what's been happening since you went to sleep? Do you jump straight on to your emails to see what crises have occurred overnight and what's waiting for you when you get into the office? Do you lie in bed thinking about your to-do list and how it seems to be getting longer every day?

How does this make you feel? Relaxed? Calm? Ready to face the day?

This is how I used to start my day; these are actual examples of what I would do every morning when I woke up. And I can tell you, it didn't make me feel relaxed, calm, or ready to face the day ahead. It used to make me feel stressed, worried, and anxious for the minefield that I would have to navigate during another stressful day. I was always starting my day on the wrong foot.

After finding mindfulness, I slowly changed the way I woke up every morning. It wasn't easy, not by a long shot. Some mornings I felt like I would physically have to restrain myself from picking up my phone despite my good intentions of trying something new.

Mindfulness for me starts long before I get into the office. I have found by starting my day right, I'm more prepared to handle the daily challenges that arise as a leader. I have tried lots of different ways to start my day, but again it's about finding what works for you. Here are some suggestions you might like to try:

Noticing: As you slowly slip into consciousness, just take a moment to notice your surroundings and what it feels like to wake up. Feel the warmth of the bed. Notice the sunlight streaming through your windows. Listen to the sounds of the house beginning to stir. Be fully present in the moment and engaged in the activity of just waking up. Allow yourself a couple of minutes to really appreciate your surroundings before you get out of bed (or reach for your phone).

Smile: When I'm thinking, I tend to have this scowl on my face, kind of like resting bitch face but not as mean! So remember as you wake up to smile, because the physical act of smiling (whether you feel like it or not) can have an impact on your thoughts and your mood. Smiling is also the perfect primer for the next suggested activity.

Gratitude: Every morning as I wake up, I list three things that I am grateful for. I try and mix it up from day to day, but sometimes the old favourites-family, my health, abundance, the miracle of life, my job-will reoccur more often than others.

Intention: It is useful first thing in the morning to set an intention for the day on how you want to show up as a person and as a leader. Do you want to be a better communicator? Spend more time with your staff? Make more time for mindfulness? Intention is something that deserves its own space, so I will write about that more in the next chapter.

Meditation: Mornings are my go-to time for my main meditation. Despite the recommendations not to, I usually stay in bed, lying down (often it's too cold to get out of bed!), and I just set a timer on my watch. Most mornings I do a basic breathing meditation, just trying to stay with my breath and noticing if any thoughts come up. If you are just starting out, you could use this time to try and stretch out your micro meditations. But don't push too far too fast!

Guided meditation: There are a lot of apps available nowadays that offer free (or paid) guided meditations. I still use guided meditations from time to time to mix up my practice or try something new. Following a short, guided meditation as you wake up is a great way to start your day.

The last thing I do before I get out of bed, as my feet hit the ground for the first time, I say to myself or out loud, 'Today is going to be a great day!' Just saying that phrase as I make my transition into the day puts me into the right frame of mind to look for the positives and not focus on the bad things that may come up.

21

Setting a Daily Intention

Although intentions are future focused, I have found that by setting an intention I can shape the experience I want for an event or day. I can check in regularly during the day and remind myself of what it is I want to focus on or experience in that moment.

I first started using intentions a couple of years ago when a few special events didn't quite go to plan. Once, after a fight with my wife about running late for dinner, I was left wondering, 'How did that happen?' We were meant to be going out for a lovely dinner together, our first night out without the kids in ages, and now we aren't even talking to each other.

Instead of being present and thinking, 'It's okay if we are little late' or 'Isn't it nice the effort she is going to for our big night out', I got caught up in my own internal monologue, 'I can't believe she is running late again' and 'why is she doing this to me'. Something I had been looking forward to for weeks was now in tatters because I wasn't focusing on what I really wanted from the evening.

Nowadays, apart from being a little more patient, I like to remind myself before an event what am I hoping for from this experience. If we are catching up with friends, it might be about connecting and enjoying the experience. If I have a special occasion planned for my boys and me, it could be to really enjoy this stage of their lives before they grow up. If I have a special meal planned, it might be to really savour the flavours of my food, or the entire dining experience. Funnily enough, since adopting this new way of doing things, my intention has never once been to be on time to a restaurant!

I also use intentions to start the workday on the right foot. Before I even get out of bed, after I have woken up and done my morning meditation, I will think about what I am trying to experience out of the day's activities. That might include being more present, being a better leader, practicing patience, laughing more, connecting with my team, being kinder to people, believing in myself, and the list goes on . . .

Setting my intention at the start of the day helps get me in the right frame of mind. Intentions can be vague, for example, to be an outstanding communicator today. But they can also be very specific, like resolving to sit down with John at lunch and check in with how he's doing because I know he's having a rough time at home. And, of course, it can be a mix-you will find what works best for you.

It's important to come back to your intentions throughout the day, so you may want to write them in your phone, on a post-it note, or on the back of your hand-that can sometimes be an interesting conversation starter!

22

Walking Mindfully

We spend a lot of time walking during the day: between meetings, back and forth to the car, shopping, bathroom breaks, while exercising, or by just walking aimlessly around the office.

What are you usually thinking about as you walk around? In most cases it's worrying about the past or thinking about the future-to-do lists, agenda items not covered, stewing over the last conversation you had with your boss, getting angry about something a co-worker said to you three weeks ago . . . This is another example of where we can be putting that time to better use!

Walking mindfully is simply paying attention and being mindful while walking. You can focus on your breath, the physical sensations around you as you walk, or you can even pay attention to your surroundings. All of these things will bring you out of your head and your never-ending thought patterns and back to the present moment.

If you are new to walking mindfully, I would suggest starting off small and working your way up to longer and more regular walks. As you become accustomed to the practice you will find it easier and more enjoyable. Try and find a walk that you do regularly throughout the day and use that as your reminder to walk mindfully.

You could also try a walking meditation. This is a more formal process of intentionally slowing down your walk and using this as the focus of your meditation. The intention isn't to get any destination; the intention is to just meditate, but instead of sitting down, you are walking around. People who can't sit still during meditation sometimes use this method because they get to move.

If you want to try this, try it in the comfort of your own home or at a park with lots of space. Take a few mindful breaths while standing in place. Slow your breathing down and notice what it's like to be standing where you are. Feel the space around you and the connection your feet make with the ground. Notice any external sensations, like the warmth of the sun or the breeze on your face.

Now take a single step. Don't just take off like a bull at a gate. Take a single, purposeful step but really try to slow down the process. Take that first step like you have never taken a step before. Notice everything. Feel the physical process of lifting your foot off the ground, propelling it forward, and then replacing it on the ground. What muscles do you feel contracting and releasing? Is there any discomfort?

Now, take another slow deliberate step. Rinse and repeat.

There is no need to walk too far, or in any particular fashion apart from keeping it slow and with awareness. Some people prefer to walk up and down a well-worn path, while others prefer to walk in a large circle so it doesn't disrupt their flow. As you get the hang of this simple process you can increase the distance or even take it on the road (not necessarily literally!).

Although I like walking meditation, I prefer to incorporate the mindful walking practice into my daily routine.

At about the time I first started trying my walking mindfully practice, I was going through a particularly tough situation at work with one of my team members. The member was having some performance issues and our conversations about those issues hadn't been going too well.

Every morning as I got out of the car at the office, my sense of unease would rapidly increase at the thought of the impending tension caused by this conflict. As I was walking into the office, I would start playing out how some of those difficult conversations might go. By the time I got to my desk, I was a mess. My stress levels had gone through the roof and all I wanted to do was turn around and go home.

I decided to use that walking time for a better purpose and focused on walking mindfully instead. As I got out of my car, instead of letting my mind wander off, I forced it to focus on my surroundings instead. What was the temperature like? Could I feel the wind on my face? Were there any smells present from the nearby flowers and trees?

As I started walking into the office, I purposefully focused my attention on the things in my immediate vicinity. By looking for novel or new things on purpose, I became curious and focused on those things instead. Isn't that a nice colour on that tree? I haven't noticed that crack in the pavement before. Aren't the warm sunrays beautiful at this time of the morning?

How do you think I felt by the time I got to my desk after using this method? It was the polar opposite to how I felt when I was pre-empting the bad things that I thought might happen in my day.

Another way you might try incorporating mindful walking into your routine is to use your bathroom breaks. It's usually a short journey that you have to do multiple times throughout the day, so it serves as a good prompt. Instead of letting your mind wander, just focus in on your surroundings and the physical process of walking.

As always, start small and try and build it this practice into a defined routine before expanding more broadly into your daily activities.

23

Time to STOP

I get asked a lot from people who are new to mindfulness about techniques they can use during stressful situations to help them calm down. They may be overwhelmed because of tight deadlines, the thought of a big presentation or dealing with a difficult conflict in the workplace.

These people don't want the long-winded answer about how they should take up a formal meditation practice or even enrol in a mindfulness course-they just need something to help them *now*, something to give them a little peace in an otherwise stressful day. I usually tell them, 'You just need to STOP!'

Using a short acronym like STOP makes it easier for us to remember, which means we are more likely to use it regularly. You can do this technique in a relatively short time frame and it really isn't that hard to remember. A lot of people I have trained over the years love this technique and have had a lot of success implementing it both at work, and at home.

It is so simple, yet so powerful.

S stands for Stop. When you become aware that you are feeling stressed or anxious about something, try and catch yourself in the act, even if you are mid-sentence or in the middle of telling yourself how awful something is. You can either say the word 'STOP' out loud or you can just say it to yourself (although, if you are talking to someone else, I would probably recommend saying it to yourself!).

T stands for Take a few breaths. Now that you have stopped, give yourself an opportunity to take a few deep, mindful breaths, focusing on inhaling through your nose and exhaling through your mouth.

O stands for Observe. You will notice as you start to breathe deeply you immediately release some of that negative tension that your negative thoughts have built up in your body. Become aware of that tension and negative energy and slowly release those too as you continue your mindful breathing. Whether you have balled up your fists, clenched your jaw, or you're just physically holding on tightly to something, it's time to let that go and breathe through it. Just observe your present experience including thoughts, feelings, and emotions without judgement.

P stands for Proceed. Allow yourself to choose the best possible way to proceed in this moment. Do you need to shake it off, make a cup of tea, or just remember that this too shall pass so you don't need to hold on so tightly? Try to take the calm you have just experienced back into the activity you are about to do next.

Just noticing that you are feeling stressed or anxious is the first step in becoming more mindful. The more regularly you use the STOP technique the better you will become at regulating your own emotions, feelings, and thoughts. You may find after a while it starts to become second nature, which is a great way of embedding your mindfulness practice into your daily routine.

Why don't you STOP now and give it a try?

24

Mono-Tasking

N owadays multitasking has become part of every busy person's modus operandi. We are always trying to do more, in less time, and are always rushing to some never-ending finish line. Unfortunately by doing multiple things at once, we aren't doing any of these tasks to the best of our ability (or even particularly well in some cases).

And, I'm sorry to say here, it doesn't matter whether you are a female or a male, the science on multi-tasking has proven that no one does it well. In fact, instead of doing multiple things at once, what we are actually doing is attention switching between the different tasks. And every time you switch tasks, there is a 0.2–0.5 second delay where your brain is in neutral. It's like what happens when you shift gears in a car-it's the time gap when the engine is idle, as you push in the clutch so that you can move from one gear to the next.

For example, in the morning you are getting yourself and the kids ready for the day ahead. You are boiling water on the stove for the eggs for number one son, while number two son prefers baked beans cooked in the microwave for the specific amount of time that ensures they meet his exacting requirements. Meanwhile, the dog is underfoot because he wants his breakfast now that everyone else is eating. Last night's dishes are still in the sink so you are trying to get those done, but unfortunately in your rush to get them done you just smashed a plate into a thousand pieces all over the kitchen floor. The toast is burning, the dog is barking, and number one son just announces that his science project that he has had for the last three weeks (but has done nothing for) is due this morning.

How mindful do you think you're feeling right now?

In our rush to get multiple things done, we don't do any one thing particularly well. To top it all off, that's usually when the negative thoughts start. Why is this always happening to me? Why do the kids always want different foods? Why do I always have to feed the dog? I'm a bad parent! Why me?

If you want a happier life, give up multi-tasking! I know that's hard to hear, and you may even think it's impossible in your particular circumstances, but I know from experience (and the research backs this up) that we should only try to focus on one thing at a time.

When we are mono-tasking we are giving our undivided attention to the task at hand, which means we can actually do it to the best of our ability. This usually means we are more efficient, more effective, and we tend to make fewer mistakes.

'Now, that's all okay in a perfect world,' I hear you say, but I'm guessing this is not going to help you get all of your jobs done. I'm going to give you a 'get out of jail free' card, because as much as I hate to admit it, I still occasionally multi-task too. Sometimes there is just no way around it and the example I used earlier in this chapter is a pretty realistic retelling of a typical weekday in my household.

But these days, for me, there's a slight difference. I slow it down and I stay mindful, especially when I notice the stress creeping in.

It's harder to be mindful when you are doing lots of things at once, but not impossible. Yes, in a perfect world I would focus on only one thing at a time, but that would require me to either get up two hours earlier every morning or employ a full-time chef/personal assistant.

So when I'm multi-tasking, I'm particularly mindful of my thoughts and my actions. I try to do less so that when something important comes up, like a profound question or comment by one of my boys, I can stop and focus entirely on that moment.

Being aware of your actions and your thoughts while you are multi-tasking is a great way of limiting damage. When my thoughts start to run away or I'm doing too many tasks, I stop myself and remember that multi-tasking is bad for my health and that I should slow down and take a few mindful breaths. Then I proceed with a smile because I know that intervention is helping to strengthen my mindfulness muscle.

25

Mindful Meetings

I have read that nine out of ten people daydream during meetings[12]. I really relate to this statistic because I am one of those nine people. And when I have looked around the room in meetings I have attended, I can tell by the look on people's faces that I am not the only one!

Meetings can be poorly organised, lack a clear direction, stray from the agenda, or be held just for the sake of having a meeting- even when there isn't anything to discuss. It's no wonder people daydream!

I am not saying all meetings are bad, I am just saying that not all meetings are created equally. If there is a specific topic, with a set agenda, and it is conducted in a timely manner (the shorter the better), meetings can actually serve an important purpose.

So how do we stay mindful during meetings and how do we encourage others to do the same? Below are some ideas you can incorporate into your next mindful meeting. You can use any or all of the suggestions, or tailor one to meet your specific needs.

Put phones away. Encourage people to turn off their phones and tablets for the duration of the meeting. In my meetings I call it 'Apples to the roof'; meaning everyone should turn their iPhone or iPad over so their Apple symbol is facing up and their screens are facing down. That sometimes causes a comment from the non-Apple people in the room, but it's a lighthearted way of asking people to not engage with their technological devices for the duration of the meeting. If you can, provide pens and paper as an alternative so people can still take notes without their devices.

Take a mindful minute. Before the meeting begins, ask everyone to take sixty seconds to just breathe and focus on being present. You can do this as a guided meditation, talking people through how to do it, or just a minute of silence.

Encourage self-monitoring. Ask people to self-monitor their attention level throughout the meeting and to just notice when their mind starts to wander. Let them know it's okay for their mind to wander, it's completely natural, but when it does they should just gently bring it back into the present moment.

Inspire gratitude. Before you start with the first agenda item, get everyone to share something they are grateful for. This doesn't have to be a long process and it can be a work thing or a personal thing, it doesn't really matter. This creates positivity within people and a sense of cohesion as people start off the meeting on the right foot. It is a way of bringing people out of their heads and into the present moment.

Start with the 'why'. Why have you called everyone here today? What is the purpose of the meeting and why is it important people have given up their valuable time to be here? Be clear about the agenda and what outcomes you are hoping to achieve. By telling people the why, you may get more buy-in, which creates more incentive to pay attention.

Take a break. Make sure you take regular breaks during meetings that last longer than an hour, just to stand up and stretch. This gets the blood pumping and allows the mind to rest between periods of heavy concentration. Encourage people to notice the different sensations they feel in their body as they move around mindfully.

Group monitoring. As the facilitator of the meeting it's important to monitor the group and to get a sense of how everyone is travelling. You should be monitoring to see if more breaks are needed, when the discussion starts to get off topic, and ensuring everyone is contributing (even the quiet people!). Summarise key points and link different topics together to show how it all fits into the stated purpose of the meeting.

Pause and reset. If the meeting runs hot, get everyone to pause for a minute and focus on their breath. This is not thinking time; this is being time. Let them know that you'll give them a chance to reflect on what has been said when you reconvene. You don't want people using the breathing time to just be preparing for the next barrage.

End the meeting mindfully. At the closing of the meeting, offer people the chance to take another mindful minute. This is an opportunity to reconnect with the breath before transitioning back into work-mode. People are sometimes reluctant to stop at the end of meetings because they just want to get back to work (or onto the next meeting), but this is a valuable opportunity to transition in a more mindful way.

It's important when implementing mindful meetings to really know your audience. In a small, receptive group, applying some or all of these techniques above could go really well. However, I would caution you in implementing all of the suggestions above in one hit, especially if you are working with larger groups. Not everyone will be receptive or will have even heard of mindfulness before. It's worthwhile having a meeting about mindfulness before you start having mindful meetings!

Check in with the group after the first couple of mindful meetings to find out how everyone is enjoying the new techniques, what's working, and what's not. Use this feedback to shape how you conduct future mindful meetings.

26

Better Decision-Making

I f you want to make better decisions, you should try making them more mindfully. Mindful decision-making is just bringing more conscious awareness to the process of how you make decisions, and what biases may be showing up for you. Many of the principles can be found in traditional decision-making theory, however, the focus of mindful decision-making is on the internal self rather than external factors. In my experience, using a combination of mindfulness and tradition decision-making tools gives the best results.

Something I learned a long time ago is that you don't make the best decision when you are in a bad (or low) mood. It's always a good practice to ask yourself how your mood might be affecting your decision-making process. Just as you should be conscious and cautious of making difficult decisions when you are in a low mood, you should also temper enthusiasm with a dose of caution. Being aware of your mood allows you to either postpone the decision-making process or just factor in how it may affect the outcome.

Mindful decision-making helps us to put things into perspective. It facilitates a better view of all angles of a decision and avoids any particular biases that may be affecting it. If we remain mindful during the process, we can sense when we are putting too much weight on a particular factor or even pretending not to notice another. Are we bowing to social or peer pressure because we are worried about what others may say? Or is it easier to not even make a decision at all because of the potential ramifications?

If we remain mindful during decision-making we ensure we aren't making the same old decisions for the same old reasons. A lot of our decision-making processes are subconscious-or very surface-level at best. This is because, of the number of decisions we have to make every day, we can't be fully conscious of every single one (particularly if they have little or no consequence). It's important, therefore, to make sure we aren't making important decisions on autopilot. Bringing more awareness to our thinking processes helps us to make better decisions every time.

Mindful decision-making also gives us the opportunity to clarify what our objectives are, for example, does this fit with my vision and long-term goals? It's taking a 'helicopter view' to help give us a wider view and a better perspective. This in turn helps us understand whether we are doing something because it's easy right now. Thinking more strategically about our decision can also prompt us to the think about the ethics involved and whether we are making a decision for the right reasons.

Being more mindful during decision-making helps us to generate not only *more* options, but *better* options. It allows us to gather more useful information rather than just relying on the same ideas generated by habitual thinking. If we are consciously seeking out information to give us a more balanced picture to work with, we are more likely to make a more informed decision.

Once the decision has been made, or even in the closing stages of the process, being more mindful allows us to become less attached to the outcome. Many people have a tendency to really want (hope) for things to turn out a certain way. The problem is that we don't always have control. One of the foundations of mindfulness is non-striving, which is learning to let go of how you think things should be. Knowing that the decision has been made and the outcome is potentially out of your hands should allow you to sleep better at night.

Finally, mindful decision-making can help us learn from failure. Being more mindful during the post-outcome phase (after the we know the results of the decision) can help you revaluate planning, preparation, and execution so you can make improved decisions the next time. Reminding yourself that certain things were out of your control, or that you did the best you could with the information you had at that time will help you to go easier on yourself when things don't turn out the way you were expecting.

27

Reflective Practice

I don't know about you, but most people I meet tell me they don't spend enough time developing themselves as leaders. For most of us, formal leadership development opportunities are few and far between. Yes, we may read the occasional leadership book (thank you very much!), but what are we doing on a regular basis to ensure we are being the best leader possible?

One of the best tools I have found over the years to develop my leadership capability is reflective practice. Reflective practice is looking back on an event or a period of time with the intention of learning from it so we can improve for next time.

Some of you may already have the start of a reflective practice, or you might have been doing something similar for years but didn't bother to define it (or you may just be calling it something different). You may do it while driving home from work, thinking about a tough conversation you had earlier in the day. You may think about a work situation that didn't go to plan while taking a shower. Or you may find the weekend walk with the dog is when you take stock of your week and think about how you could have done things better. These are all forms of informal reflective practice.

A more formal style would include making notes or keeping a journal. I'm not talking about writing in your diary like a twelve-year-old schoolgirl; I'm talking about making notes about conversations, interactions or thoughts/feelings about the trials and tribulations of being a leader. It's crucial to think about our past failures, mistakes, and successes in a way that helps us to learn from these events.

So how do we do it?

Firstly, it's best to find a quiet place where you can write comfortably and won't be interrupted regularly. The experts say that using good old-fashioned paper and pen is best, but if you prefer to use a laptop, tablet, or phone, do whatever works for you!

I also recommend not reflecting on a situation that has just happened. Often when things are still raw there are a lot of emotions festering within us so it's hard to stay objective. Give yourself a little space from the situation and allow yourself to calm down before spending any time reflecting on it.

Next, choose the situation or topic that you want to reflect on. Try not to be too broad here; we aren't trying to solve all of your leadership dilemmas in one foul swoop. Often we reflect on negative experiences because there are stronger emotions involved, but we can absolutely learn from positive experiences as well.

Start writing a description of the event or situation-try to remain as objective as possible. Some people prefer free form, where they just start writing and see what bubbles to the surface. There is no structure here, just write down what comes to mind, but keep the overall goal in mind: what can I learn from this situation so I can do it better next time?

Others prefer a more structured, formal approach. For those people, I recommend the Gibbs reflective cycle. The Gibbs reflective cycle is a series of steps that help you step through the situation by providing a series of prompts for you to consider.

When it comes to reflective practice, it's important to remember that you don't want to overdo it. It's useful to reflect on a situation to try and learn from it, but if we keep going over and over it in our heads it quickly becomes rumination (this is where being mindful helps!). I have found over the years that after I have reflected on a situation once, it's best to let it go and move on.

This is an easy practice to start today, remembering that the more you do it, the more effective you will become. Over the years I've developed my own style, which is a mixture of the more formal approach and just jotting down whatever comes to mind. By sticking to a regular reflective practice, we will constantly be able to assess our actions and leadership and then self-correct where necessary.

28

Transitions

Transitioning between your activities is a way of being more conscious as you move from one thing to the next. This could be between multiple meetings at work, or going from lunch time back into work time, or transitioning after holidays back into work.

One transition that I know is vital in my life is the transition between work and home. It is so important to me because it allows me to decompress from a stressful day and to be truly present for the most important people in my life: my family.

Work and home tend to have different rhythms, and unless you make the conscious choice, you can find yourself a major disruption to the family unit. This is particularly noticeable for me when I walk in the door after my workday is done. It doesn't matter whether I am in the best mood or the worst, there is no way of knowing what is behind that door as I walk into my house (it's kind of like a game show 'Let's see what's behind door number one!'). If I don't show up in the right frame of mind and with the energy my family deserves, things can go a little pear shaped.

There is a great TED talk by Dr Adam Fraser about transitioning which he calls 'The Third Space'[13]. He talks about a CEO colleague of his who has actually built another entrance to his house so that he can ensure he doesn't disrupt the family rhythm as he arrives home. The entrance is built so he can enter the house discreetly and directly to his bedroom where he has a shower, puts on some casual clothes, and gets out of 'CEO mode'. This allows him to then greet his family in a better frame of mind.

Now, as wonderful as that sounds, most of us can't afford to build a separate entrance to our house. I can't even sneak around the back to try and slip up the stairs to my room because the dog would alert the rest of the house I'm home anyway!

When I talk about transitioning between work and home with participants on my leadership programs, most people agree the car ride home is often the only option to try and take a breath before engaging with the family. For them, this means listening to music, thinking about their day, engaging in mindful driving, or chatting with friends or colleagues on their hands-free smartphone.

For me, if I'm not practicing mindful driving, I will usually listen to music, an audiobook, or podcast most of the way home. But I know there is a set of traffic lights about five minutes from my house, and that is when I switch off whatever it is I'm doing as I prepare to enter into 'home mode'. I do not allow myself to think about my workday or what things need to be done the next day. My sole focus is on mentally preparing myself to show up mindfully for my family as soon as I walk in the door.

Those five minutes aren't always the same routine. For example, I may think about how I want to show up when I walk in the door, what things my family may have been doing during the day that I want to ask them about, or I might remind myself how grateful I am to be coming home to such an amazing family.

This simple change of focus and mental preparation means I arrive home ready to give my family the energy and attention they deserve. It puts me in a better frame of mind and focuses my attention so that when I walk in that door, I'm ready for game time!

IV

What Next?

Embodying mindful leadership

29

Leadership Legacy

A useful exercise you should do every so often is to contemplate what sort of legacy you want to leave behind as a leader. How do you want to be remembered? What contribution do you want to make to your team, the organisation, or to the community?

Creating a vision of what that looks like will be your northern light to help guide you on your leadership journey. Particularly on the tough days when you aren't enjoying the work or things aren't going well with the team, it will serve to remind you of who you are as a leader, and why you have chosen to lead.

I have been lucky enough to work with some great leaders throughout my career and one in particular really made me think about what I would like my legacy to be. She wanted to be remembered as a leader who opened doors for people. Her personal mission was to see how she could create opportunities for others through her connections or by staying alert to opportunities that matched those people's goals. That included career opportunities, professional development, or even areas of personal interest.

I remember listening to her talking about her legacy one day in class and realising how much it moved and inspired her. I have been fortunate on a number of occasions to be on the receiving end of her generosity so I will certainly remember her in that light.

My leadership legacy is to help people find their path, whatever that looks like for them. When I come into a team I always want to know what really inspires people and what they would be doing if that could be anything. Then I know how I can best help them work towards getting there. Those opportunities don't have to be within our team or even our organisation, it can be something completely out of left field. I know people are at the best when they are doing what they love and they are truly connected to their mission.

Instead of just reflecting on your ideal legacy now as you read, I want you to write it down. It's important to put this in a journal, notebook or anywhere you can come back to at a later date. That way you will have a point of reference to remind you of the leader you want to be.

If you are stuck, think of other leaders you have known or who have inspired you from a distance. What was great about their leadership? What caused them to come to mind? How might you use that to find your own path and create a legacy that you can be proud of?

30

Setbacks and Other Hiccups

After reading this book, you have all the tools and techniques you need to create a more mindful leadership practice and a more mindful life. Hopefully there are even some things that you have started to implement and you are starting to notice a difference.

But what happens when the wheels come off your mindfulness practice? What if you were really starting to get the hang of some of the principles, but someone said something that rubbed you the wrong way and you couldn't help yourself, you just reacted? You had the best of intentions but being more mindful went straight out the window.

Stuff happens; it's how you get back up on the horse after being knocked off that matters most. There will always be minor setbacks that threaten to derail your whole mindfulness practice. But you have to commit to yourself right now, that no matter what happens, you will keep going. You are a human, you are going to make mistakes, but don't let those minor hiccups get in the way of your goal of becoming more mindful.

It's like when a baby is first learning to walk; every time the baby falls over you don't scold them and tell them they can't do it. You get excited for them for even trying and you encourage them to try again. You pull funny faces and you clap and cheer after every false start and every misstep. Gradually, they start to get it, slowly and a little unsteady at first, but as time goes by they become a toddler. As they mature, they get even better at walking, but they still may fall down from time to time. No one is immune to the occasional fall-even us adults!

On my own journey to be coming more mindful, I have had many setbacks, sometimes daily, sometimes several times in the same day! But no matter what happens, after I calm down and I have reflected on my actions, I just come back to being mindful. I know the benefits of mindfulness and I know I'm not always going to get it right and that's okay.

Even to this day I have setbacks where I react in a way that is not very mindful. Mindfulness is not a panacea that's going to 'fix' you. But you will become more conscious of those hiccups and, over time, grow less prone to having them.

It's also the same for meditation. It doesn't matter how many times your thoughts wander (and they will wander) it's recognising that you have lost focus, then gently bringing your attention back to the breath. When you notice you aren't being mindful, that's awesome because now you can do something about it. Noticing is half the battle, so celebrate those successes!

It's really important that you don't get too down on yourself when things go wrong. These things are going to happen, and it is not uncommon in people who are starting to learn to be mindful or meditate. Give yourself a break and treat yourself with loving kindness. Take a couple of breaths and re-commit to the practice-keeping the long-term benefits in mind, those benefits are worth the short-term setbacks.

Get Started Today

So we have come to the end of the book! Hopefully you are feeling empowered to become a more mindful leader. Hopefully I have dispelled some of the myths out there so you are more comfortable with the concepts around mindful leadership. You now have all the tools and techniques you need to start a regular mindful leadership practice at work.

The most effective way to do this is to start today while it's fresh and put an action plan in place to make it a habit. One of my favourite sayings over the last couple of years has been one percent theory, ninety-nine percent practice. I have an old habit of wanting to read more articles or find another book in a never-ending quest to absorb more information. But at the end of the day, that's not what's going to make me a more mindful leader. The only way to do that is to put what you've learnt so far in to practice, and then reflect on what's working for you.

If you haven't already picked a few of your favourite practices and started a daily routine, it's time to decide now. I recommend starting small and then working your way onto the next practice once the first is embedded. It's too easy to get overwhelmed and give up if you go too hard too quickly!

Get some support. If you haven't already, reach out to peers, colleagues or people online who are already on the mindful leadership journey so you can share with each other what's working well and what isn't.

What I have covered in this book is really just the tip of the iceberg, there is so much more to learn about being a mindful leader. I have included in the back of this book some reading suggestions you might like to check out. Being a mindful leader is a journey, and a practice. It's something you have to invest in if you truly want to embody mindful leadership.

And finally if you want some clarification around any of the topics in this book, or if you are looking for further help or resources, then please reach out to me on my website at www.robhills.com.au. I would love to help in any way I can.

About the Author

Rob Hills is a recovering over-thinker who has been practicing mindfulness for over 20 years. Rob is the author of the book *The Mindful Leadership Blueprint*. He writes in a pragmatic way to help even the skeptics discover the benefits of mindful leadership. Rob has developed a set of mindfulness techniques over the years which he teaches to others to help improve their leadership style. Rob's mission in life is to help as many people as he can learn how to lead themselves and others, through self-awareness and mindfulness. This is his first book.

You can connect with Rob at www.robhills.com.au.

Reading List

10% Happier - How I Tamed the Voice in My Head, Reduced Stress without Losing My Edge, and Found Self-help That Actually Works: A True Story - **Dan Harris**

Don't Sweat the Small Stuff And It's All Small Stuff - Simple Ways to Keep the Little Things from Taking Over Your Life - **Richard Carlson**

Finding the Space to Lead: A Practical Guide to Mindful Leadership - **Janice Marturano**

Know Yourself, Forget Yourself - Five Truths to Transform Your Work, Relationship and Everyday Life - **Marc Lesser**

Leading Change - **John P. Kotter**

Search Inside Yourself - The Unexpected Path to Achieving Success, Happiness (and World Peace) - **Chade-Meng Tan**

The Mind of the Leader - How to Lead Yourself, Your People, and Your Organization for Extraordinary Results

- **Rasmus Hougaard and Jacqueline Carter**

The Mindful Leader - 7 Practices for Transforming Your Leadership, Your Organisation and Your Life - **Michael Bunting**

The Mindful Leader: Ten Principles for Bringing Out the Best in Ourselves and Others - **Michael Carroll**

The Power of Habit - Why We Do What We Do in Life and Business - **Charles Duhigg**

Wherever You Go, There You Are - *Mindfulness Meditation in Everyday Life* - **Jon Kabat-Zinn**

Notes

WHAT IS MINDFUL LEADERSHIP?

1   Kabat-Zinn J.Wherever You Go, There You Are: Mindfulness Meditation in Everyday Life. New York, USA: Hyperion, 1994.

2   Scott S. Fierce Conversations: Achieving Success at Work and in Life One Conversation at a Time. New York, USA: Berkley, 2004.

SELF-AWARENESS

3   Goleman D. Emotional Intelligence: Why It Can Matter More Than IQ. New York: Bantam Books, 1995.

THRIVING ON BUSY

4   Parasuraman R. (1979). Memory load and event rate control sensitivity decrements in sustained attention. Science 1979;205: 924-7.

REDUCING STRESS IN THE WORKPLACE

5   Fink G. Stress: The health epidemic of the 21st century. SciTechConnect: 2016. Viewed 2 August 2018. <http://scitechconnect.elsevier.com/stress-health-epidemic-21st-century/>.

6   Goyal M, Singh S, Sibinga EM, Gould NF, Rowland-Seymour A, Sharma R, et al. Meditation programs for psychological stress and well-being: a systematic review and meta-analysis. JAMA 2014; 174(3):357–368.

7   Hughes JW, Fresco DM, Myerscough R, van Dulmen MH, Carlson LE, Josephson R. Randomised controlled trial of mindfulness-based stress reduction for prehypertension. Psychosom Med 2013; 75(8):721-8.

8   Bergland C. 10 Ways Mindfulness and Meditation Promote Well-Being. Psychology Today: 2015. Viewed 2 August 2018. <https://www.psycholo gytoday.com/us/blog/the-athletes-way/201504/10-ways-mindfulness-and-
    meditation-promote-well-being>.

REMAINING MINDFUL DURING CONFLICT

9   Covey S. 7 Habits of Highly Effective People. Anniversary Edition. USA: Franklin Covey on Brilliance Audio, 2015;247.

TECHNOLOGY TAKEOVER

10   Asurion. Are You Addicted to Your Phone?. Based on 2018 Consumer Tech Dependency Survey. Asurion: 2018. Viewed 2 August 2018. < https://www.asurion.com/connect/tech-tips/are-you-addicted-to-your-phone/>.

11   Bajarin B. Apple's Penchant for Consumer Security. Tech Pinions: 2016. Viewed 2 August 2018. <https://techpinions.com/apples-penchant-for-consumer-security/45122>.

MINDFUL MEETINGS

12   Wetmore Dr D, 9 out of 10 People Daydream During Meetings. ProMeet: 2013. Viewed 2 August 2018. <http://www.meeting-facilitation.co.uk/ blog/files/9-out-of-10-people-daydream-in-meetings.html>.

TRANSITIONS

13   TEDx Talks.Three simple steps to not take a bad day home. YouTube. TEDx Talks: 2015. Viewed 2 August 2018. <https://www.youtube.com/ channel/UCsT0YIqwnpJCM-mx7-gSA4Q>.